WORD PLAY!
WRITE YOUR OWN
CRAZY COMICS
#1

CHUCK WHELON

DOVER PUBLICATIONS, INC.
MINEOLA, NEW YORK

NOTE

Use your imagination to fill the speech balloons in this delightful book with your own clever dialogue. Look at the panels for each comic and get the story line, and then come up with the words. You'll find scenes at a baseball game, a carnival, and in a jungle, and you'll encounter a dragon, a frog princess, a mummy, a UFO, and even Frankenstein. Enjoy creating your own comics with these memorable characters and settings—and many more!

Copyright

Copyright © 2011, 2013 by Dover Publications, Inc.
All rights reserved.

Bibliographical Note

Boost Word Play! Write Your Own Crazy Comics #1, first published by Dover Publications, Inc., in 2013, is a revised edition of *Word Play! Write Your Own Crazy Comics #1,* originally published by Dover in 2011.

International Standard Book Number

ISBN-13: 978-0-486-49441-8
ISBN-10: 0-486-49441-1

Manufactured in the United States by Courier Corporation
49441101   2013
www.doverpublications.com

ART MUSEUM

CCSS W.3.2.a Introduce a topic and group related information together; include illustrations when useful to aiding comprehension. Also **W.3.2.d, L.3.3.a; W.4.2.a, W.4.2.e, L.4.3.a; W.5.2.a, W.5.2.e, L.5.2.d.**

BABYSITTER

CCSS W.3.3.a Establish a situation and introduce a narrator and/or characters; organize an event sequence that unfolds naturally. Also **W.3.3.b, L.3.3.b; W.4.3.a, W.4.3.e, L.4.3.b; W.5.3.a, W.5.3.e, L.5.3.b.**

BAKING

BASEBALL

CCSS W.3.3.b Use dialogue and descriptions of actions, thoughts, and feelings to develop experiences and events or show the response of characters to situations. Also **W.3.3.d, L.3.3.b, L.3.6; W.4.3.b, W.4.3.e, L.4.3.b, L.4.6; W.5.3.b, W.5.3.e, L.5.6.**

BASKETBALL

BBQ

CCSS W.3.1.a Introduce the topic or text they are writing about, state an opinion, and create an organizational structure that lists reasons. Also **W.3.1.d, L.3.6; W.4.1.a, W.4.1.d, L.4.6; W.5.1.a, W.5.1.d, L.5.6.**

BIG FOOT

CCSS W.3.3.a Establish a situation and introduce a narrator and/or characters; organize an event sequence that unfolds naturally. Also **W.3.3.b, L.3.6; W.4.3.a, W.4.3.b, L.4.6; W.5.3.a, L.5.6.**

BIRTHDAY GIRL

BOWLING

CCSS W.3.3.a Establish a situation and introduce a narrator and/or characters; organize an event sequence that unfolds naturally. Also **W.3.3.b, L.3.3.a; W.4.3.a, W.4.3.b, L.4.3.a, L.4.3.b; W.5.3.a, W.5.3.b, L.5.3.**

CAFETERIA

CCSS W.3.3.c Use temporal words and phrases to signal event order. Also **W.3.3.a, W.3.3.b, W.3.3.d; W.4.3.a, W.4.3.b, W.4.3.c, W.4.3.e; W.5.3.a, W.5.3.c, W.5.3.e.**

CAMEL RACE

CAR

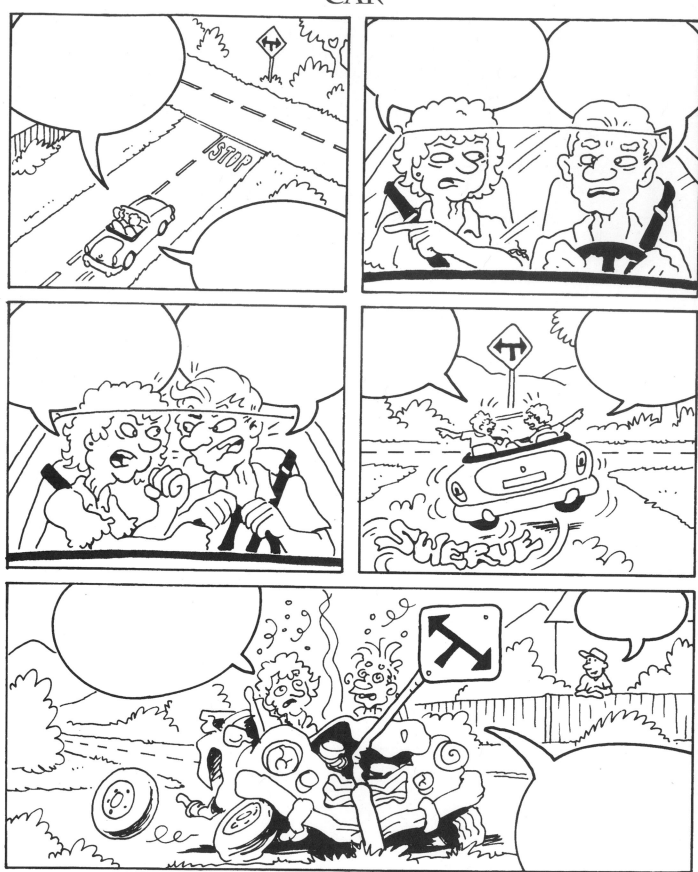

CCSS W.3.1.a Introduce the topic or text they are writing about, state an opinion, and create an organizational structure that lists reasons. Also **W.3.1.d, L.3.3.b; W.4.1.a, W.4.1.d, L.4.3.b; W.5.1.b, L.5.3.**

CARNIVAL PRIZE

CCSS W.3.3.b Use dialogue and descriptions of actions, thoughts, and feelings to develop experiences and events or show the response of characters to situations. Also **W.3.3.d, L.3.3.b; W.4.3.b, W.4.3.e, L.4.3.b; W.5.3.b, W.5.3.e, L.5.3.**

CARNIVAL RIDE

CCSS **W.3.1.a** Introduce the topic or text they are writing about, state an opinion, and create an organizational structure that lists reasons. Also **W.3.1.b, W.3.1.d; W.4.1.a, W.4.1.b, W.4.1.d; W.5.1.a, W.5.1.b, W.5.1.d.**

CLOWNS

COMPUTER

CCSS **W.3.3.b** Use dialogue and descriptions of actions, thoughts, and feelings to develop experiences and events or show the response of characters to situations. Also **W.3.3.d, L.3.3.a; W.4.3.b, W.4.3.e, L.4.3.a, L.4.3.c; W.5.3.b, W.5.3.e, L.5.3.b.**

CURFEW

CCSS W.3.3.a Establish a situation and introduce a narrator and/or characters; organize an event sequence that unfolds naturally. Also **W.3.3.b, W.3.3.c; W.4.3.a, W.4.3.b, W.4.3.c; W.5.3.a, W.5.3.b, W.5.3.c.**

DESERT

 W.3.3.d Provide a sense of closure. Also W.3.3.b, L.3.3.b; W.4.3.b, W.4.3.d, W.4.3.e, L.4.3.c; W.5.3.b, W.5.3.d, W.5.3.e, L.5.3.b.

DINER

CCSS W.3.3.a Establish a situation and introduce a narrator and/or characters; organize an event sequence that unfolds naturally. Also **W.3.3.b, L.3.3.a; W.4.3.a, W.4.3.b, L.4.3.a, L.4.3.b; W.5.3.a, W.5.3.b, L.5.3.**

DOGFIGHT

CCSS W.3.3.b Use dialogue and descriptions of actions, thoughts, and feelings to develop experiences and events or show the response of characters to situations. Also **W.3.3.c, L.3.3.a; W.4.3.b, W.4.3.c, L.4.3.a, L.4.3.b; W.5.3.b, W.5.3.c.**

DOG WALK

CCSS W.3.3.a Establish a situation and introduce a narrator and/or characters; organize an event sequence that unfolds naturally. Also **W.3.3.b, W.3.3.d; W.4.3.a, W.4.3.b, W.4.3.e; W.5.3.a, W.5.3.b, W.5.3.e.**

DRAGON

 W.3.3.b Use dialogue and descriptions of actions, thoughts, and feelings to develop experiences and events or show the response of characters to situations. Also W.3.3.d, L.3.3.a; W.4.3.b, W.4.3.e, L.4.3.a, L.4.3.c; W.5.3.b, W.5.3.e, L.5.3.b.

EAGLE

CCSS W.3.3.a Establish a situation and introduce a narrator and/or characters; organize an event sequence that unfolds naturally. Also **W.3.3.b, W.3.3.d, L.3.6; W.4.3.a, W.4.3.b, W.4.3.e, L.4.6; W.5.3.a, W.5.3.b, W.5.3.e, L.5.6.**

FIREFLIES

CCSS W.3.3.c Use temporal words and phrases to signal event order. Also **W.3.3.a, W.3.3.b, W.3.3.d; W.4.3.a, W.4.3.b, W.4.3.e; W.5.3.a, W.5.3.b, W.5.3.e.**

FRANKENSTEIN

CCSS W.3.3.b Use dialogue and descriptions of actions, thoughts, and feelings to develop experiences and events or show the response of characters to situations. Also **W.3.3.c, L.3.3.a; W.4.3.b, W.4.3.c, L.4.3.a, L.4.3.b; W.5.3.b, W.5.3.c, L.5.6.**

FROG PRINCESS

CCSS W.3.3.a Establish a situation and introduce a narrator and/or characters; organize an event sequence that unfolds naturally. Also **W.3.3.b, L.3.3.a; W.4.3.a, W.4.3.b, L.4.3.a, L.4.3.c; W.5.3.a, W.5.3.b, L.5.3.b.**

GIFT

CCSS W.3.3.d Provide a sense of closure. Also W.3.3.b, L.3.3.a; W.4.3.b, W.4.3.e, L.4.3.a, L.4.3.b; W.5.3.b, W.5.3.e.

HOMEWORK

CCSS W.3.3.a Establish a situation and introduce a narrator and/or characters; organize an event sequence that unfolds naturally. Also **W.3.3.b; W.4.3.a, W.4.3.b; W.5.3.a, W.5.3.b.**

HORSE

CCSS W.3.3.b Use dialogue and descriptions of actions, thoughts, and feelings to develop experiences and events or show the response of characters to situations. Also **W.3.3.a, W.3.3.d, L.3.3.a; W.4.3.b, W.4.3.e, L.4.3.a, L.4.3.b; W.5.3.b, W.5.3.e.**

JUNGLE

CCSS W.3.3.a Establish a situation and introduce a narrator and/or characters; organize an event sequence that unfolds naturally. Also **W.3.3.b, W.3.3.d; W.4.3.a, W.4.3.b, W.4.3.e; W.5.3.a, W.5.3.b, W.5.3.e.**

ICE CREAM

CCSS W.3.3.c Use temporal words and phrases to signal event order. Also **W.3.3.a, W.3.3.b, L.3.3.a; W.4.3.a, W.4.3.b, L.4.3.a, L.4.3.b; W.5.3.a, W.5.3.b.**

MOON

CCSS   **W.3.1.a** Introduce the topic or text they are writing about, state an opinion, and create an organizational structure that lists reasons. Also **W.3.1.d, L.3.3.a; W.4.1.d, L.4.3.a, L.4.3.b; W.5.1.a, W.5.1.d.**

MOVIE THEATER

CCSS **W.3.3.b** Use dialogue and descriptions of actions, thoughts, and feelings to develop experiences and events or show the response of characters to situations. Also **W.3.3.a, W.3.3.c; W.4.3.a, W.4.3.b, W.4.3.c; W.5.3.a, W.5.3.b, W.5.3.c.**

NESSIE

CCSS W.3.3.a Establish a situation and introduce a narrator and/or characters; organize an event sequence that unfolds naturally. Also **W.3.3.b, W.3.3.d, L.3.3.b; W.4.3.a, W.4.3.b, W.4.3.e, L.4.3.c; W.5.3.a, W.5.3.b, W.5.3.e, L.5.3.b.**

MUMMY

MUSIC ROOM

CCSS W.3.3.a Establish a situation and introduce a narrator and/or characters; organize an event sequence that unfolds naturally. Also W.3.3.b, W.3.3.d; W.4.3.b, W.4.3.d, L.4.3.b; W.5.3.b, W.5.3.e.

PAINTING

CCSS W.3.1.a Introduce the topic or text they are writing about, state an opinion, and create an organizational structure that lists reasons. Also W.3.1.d, L.3.3.a; W.4.1.a, W.4.1.d, L.4.3.a, L.4.3.b; W.5.1.a, W.5.1.d.

PARTY DRESS

PHOTOGRAPHER

GRAND CANYON

CCSS W.3.3.d Provide a sense of closure. Also W.3.3.b, L.3.3.a; W.4.3.b, W.4.3.e, L.4.3.a, L.4.3.b; W.5.3.b, W.5.3.e, L.5.3.

PIRATES

PLANE

CCSS W.3.3.b Use dialogue and descriptions of actions, thoughts, and feelings to develop experiences and events or show the response of characters to situations. Also **W.3.3.d, L.3.6; W.4.3.b, W.4.3.e, L.4.6; W.5.3.b, W.5.3.e, L.5.6.**

PLAY

POLE VAULT

CCSS W.3.3.b Use dialogue and descriptions of actions, thoughts, and feelings to develop experiences and events or show the response of characters to situations. Also **W.3.3.d, L.3.3.a; W.4.3.b, W.4.3.e, L.4.3.a; W.5.3.b, W.5.3.e, L.5.3.**

POOL SHARK

CCSS W.3.3.c Use temporal words and phrases to signal event order. Also **W.3.3.a, W.3.3.b, W.3.3.d, L.3.3.a; W.4.3.a, W.4.3.b, W.4.3.e, L.4.3.a, L.4.6; W.5.3.a, W.5.3.b, W.5.3.e.**

SKATEBOARD

CCSS W.3.3.d Provide a sense of closure. Also **W.3.3.a, W.3.3.b, W.3.3.d; W.4.3.a, W.4.3.b, W.4.3.e; W.5.3.a, W.5.3.b, W.5.3.e.**

SANDCASTLE

CCSS W.3.3.b Use dialogue and descriptions of actions, thoughts, and feelings to develop experiences and events or show the response of characters to situations. Also **W.3.3.d, L.3.6; W.4.3.b, W.4.3.e, L.4.6; W.5.3.b, W.5.3.e, L.5.6.**

SCARY MOVIE

SKIING

CCSS W.3.1.a Introduce the topic or text they are writing about, state an opinion, and create an organizational structure that lists reasons. Also **W.3.1.b, W.3.1.d, L.3.3.a; W.4.1.a, W.4.1.b, W.4.1.d, L.4.3.a; W.5.1.a, W.5.1.b, W.5.1.d.**

SNACK

CCSS **W.3.3.b** Use dialogue and descriptions of actions, thoughts, and feelings to develop experiences and events or show the response of characters to situations. Also **W.3.3.d, L.3.6; W.4.3.b, W.4.3.e, L.4.6; W.5.3.b, W.5.3.e, L.5.6.**

SNORKELERS

CCSS W.3.3.c Use temporal words and phrases to signal event order. Also **W.3.3.a, W.3.3.b, L.3.3.a; W.4.3.a, W.4.3.b, W.4.3.c, L.4.3.a, L.4.3.b; W.5.3.a, W.5.3.b, W.5.3.c, L.5.3.**

STRONGMAN

CCSS **W.3.1.a** Introduce the topic or text they are writing about, state an opinion, and create an organizational structure that lists reasons. Also **W.3.1.b, L.3.3.a; W.4.1.a, W.4.1.b, L.4.3.a; W.5.1.a, W.5.1.b, W.5.1.d.**

SUPERMARKET

CCSS W.3.3.b Use dialogue and descriptions of actions, thoughts, and feelings to develop experiences and events or show the response of characters to situations. Also **W.3.3.d, L.3.6; W.4.3.b, W.4.3.e, L.4.6; W.5.3.b, W.5.3.e, L.5.6.**

SURFERS

CCSS W.3.3.c Use temporal words and phrases to signal event order. Also **W.3.3.a, W.3.3.b, W.3.3.d; W.4.3.a, W.4.3.b, W.4.3.e; W.5.3.a, W.5.3.b, W.5.3.e.**

UFO

CCSS W.3.3.b Use dialogue and descriptions of actions, thoughts, and feelings to develop experiences and events or show the response of characters to situations. Also **W.3.3.a, L.3.3.a; W.4.3.a, W.4.3.b, W.4.3.e, L.4.3.a, L.4.3.b; W.5.3.a, W.5.3.b, L.5.3.**

UMBRELLA

CCSS W.3.3.a Establish a situation and introduce a narrator and/or characters; organize an event sequence that unfolds naturally. Also W.3.3.b, W.3.3.c; W.4.3.a, W.4.3.b, W.4.3.c, W.4.3.d; W.5.3.a, W.5.3.b, W.5.3.c, W.5.3.d, W.5.3.e.

WEREWOLF

CCSS W.3.3.b Use dialogue and descriptions of actions, thoughts, and feelings to develop experiences and events or show the response of characters to situations. Also **W.3.3.d, L.3.3.a; W.4.3.b, W.4.3.e, L.4.3.a, L.4.3.b; W.5.3.b, W.5.3.e.**

WRONG DOOR

CCSS W.3.3.c Use temporal words and phrases to signal event order. Also W.3.3.a, W.3.3.b, W.3.3.d; W.4.3.a; W.4.3.b, W.4.3.e, L.4.3.b; W.5.3.a, W.5.3.b, W.5.3.e.

"XTRA" SCARY STORY

CCSS **W.3.3.b** Use dialogue and descriptions of actions, thoughts, and feelings to develop experiences and events or show the response of characters to situations. Also **W.3.3.d, L.3.3.a; W.4.3.b, W.4.3.d, W.4.3.e, L.4.3.a, L.4.3.b; W.5.3.b, W.5.3.e, L.5.3.**